LAZY REVOLUTION

The Art of Conscious Laziness and
the Power of Doing Less

by
Harry L. Nikula

For those who dare to rest.
This revolution begins with a pause.

© 2025 Harry L. Nikula

All rights reserved.

No part of this publication may be reproduced, stored in a retrieval system, or transmitted in any form or by any means — electronic, mechanical, photocopying, recording or otherwise — without the prior written permission of the author.

Paperback: 978-1-9193053-0-1
Hardback: 978-1-9193053-1-8
eBook: 978-1-9193053-2-5

First Edition, 2025

Published by Harry L. Nikula

Printed in the United Kingdom

A Lazy Revolution Original

This book is a work of creative non-fiction. Names, characters, and events have been used for illustrative purposes. Any resemblance to real persons, living or dead, is purely coincidental.

Contents

Introduction: Under the Lazy Sun 1

Chapter 1: The Myth of the Lazy – Who Decided It Was Wrong to Sit Still? 5

Chapter 2: Good Laziness vs. Harmful Laziness 11

Chapter 3: The Science of Slowing Down 17

Chapter 4: What History's Geniuses Really Knew About Laziness . 23

Chapter 5: Laziness as a Survival Skill 27

Chapter 6: The Art of Doing Nothing Without Guilt 33

Chapter 7: Afternoon Naps – The Secret Power Source 37

Chapter 8: Dress Simple, Think Less 43

Chapter 9: Minimal Accessories, Maximum Freedom 47

Chapter 10: Eat, Rest, Repeat – A Lazy Approach to Food 51

Chapter 11: Move Like a Lazy Genius: Effort, Ease and Energy 55

Chapter 12: Lazy Communication: Saying More by Talking Less 61

Chapter 13: Digital Laziness: Controlling Tech Before It Controls You 67

Chapter 14: The Lazy Approach to Work: Results Without the Rush 73

Chapter 15: Money the Lazy Way: Simplifying Finances 79

Chapter 16: Relationships Made Easy: Love Without Overcomplication 83

Chapter 17: The Wisdom of Waiting: Patience as a Lazy Virtue 87

Chapter 18: Positive Procrastination: Why Not Everything Must Be Urgent 91

Chapter 19: Creative Laziness: Innovation Through Doing Less 97

Chapter 20: The Lazy Traveler: Seeing the World Without Stress .. 103

Chapter 21: Lazy Parenting: Raising Kids Without Burnout 107

Chapter 22: The Lazy Leader: Guiding Without Micromanaging .. 111

Chapter 23: Society and the Lazy Revolution: Rethinking Productivity Culture 115

Chapter 24: Lazy Nirvana: Gratitude in Stillness 119

Chapter 25: The Future Belongs to the Lazy: A New Vision for Living 123

Bonus Chapter X: The Gentle Art of Indulgence: A Glass of Good Wine 129

Bonus Chapter Y: If You Laze, Laze in Style: The Soundtrack of Conscious Laziness 133

Bonus Chapter Z: The Shady Principle: Better £5 in the Shade Than £10 in the Sun 137

- The Language of the Lazy 141
- The Conscious Lazy Manifesto 144
- Final Words 147
- **Epilogue:** The Power of Doing Less 149

Introduction

Under the Lazy Sun

I am forty-five years old, and I've lived two lives under the same sun. In one, I was the overachiever — organised, efficient, permanently out of breath. In the other, I became the conscious lazy — slower, lighter, quietly productive.

Between those two worlds lies this book.

I still remember one morning, standing half-awake in my own kitchen, realising I'd become everything I once admired and nothing I actually liked.

My calendar was full, my mind was empty, and I hadn't watched a sunrise without checking emails in years.

That quiet awareness didn't feel like defeat — it felt like the first honest pause in a very long time.

I've been a twelve-year-old worker, a sixteen-year-old employee, a manager, a self-employed craftsman, a CEO, an entrepreneur.

I've known alarm clocks that bite, deadlines that stretch into weekends, and that persistent whisper: *"Do more, or you'll fall behind."*

But I've also known naps that saved afternoons, simple meals that felt like philosophy, and mornings when dressing quickly meant thinking clearly.

Somewhere along the way, I realised that **the art of doing less is the only sustainable form of doing more.**

Why Write About Laziness?

Because we've been lied to — elegantly, repeatedly, and since childhood.

Teachers rewarded haste, not understanding.

Bosses mistook hours for loyalty.

Society taught us to worship fatigue as proof of value.

Yet many of the minds we admire most — from scientists to poets to inventors — were masters of deliberate idleness.

Bill Gates isolates himself twice a year to think.

Warren Buffett spends most of his day reading.

Even the modern neuroscience of focus (thank you, Andrew Huberman) confirms what our bodies always knew: *rest refuels intelligence.*

If laziness was a flaw, evolution would have erased it.

Instead, it preserved it — as wisdom disguised as weakness.

From Busy to Conscious

I've lived both extremes:

The man who colour-codes his calendar to extract every drop of efficiency, and the man who simply refuses to hurry.

The first achieved goals.

The second discovered meaning.

True laziness — conscious, gentle, lucid — is not inertia.

It's clarity.

It's knowing that motion is only progress when it leads somewhere worth arriving.

What This Book Isn't

This is not a self-help manual.

It won't shout "Ten Steps to a Slower You."

You'll find humour, a few studies, a touch of philosophy, and several naps' worth of reflection.

It's not about giving up on effort — it's about re-imagining effort itself.

You'll learn to value ease, design simplicity, rest without guilt, and choose quality over chaos.

If the modern world runs on caffeine and anxiety, *Lazy Revolution* runs on oxygen and irony.

The Lazy Manifesto in a Sentence

You're not lazy.

You're simply tired of pretending to be a machine.

So, this book gives you permission to stop running for a while — to sit under your own lazy sun and see what happens when you no longer chase it.

Lazy Exercise #0 – Permission Granted

Take a moment — no timer, no app.
Do absolutely nothing for sixty seconds.
If that feels too long, do thirty.
If that feels too short, do nothing again later.
This isn't a warm-up. It's the point.

[Lazy Dialogue →]

You've rested your attention. Now let's question the myth that made you feel guilty for it.

"Men have become the tools of their tools."
— Henry David Thoreau

"What if laziness isn't the absence of effort, but the art of choosing where effort truly matters."
— Harry L. Nikula

Chapter 1

The Myth of the Lazy – Who Decided It Was Wrong to Sit Still?

Let's start with a scandalous confession: laziness is not the problem. Laziness is the scapegoat.

For centuries, we've been told that stillness is suspicious, rest is weakness, and motion — any motion — is proof of worth.

I used to believe that too.

Whenever I sat down with no task at hand, a strange panic appeared — as if the walls themselves were watching.

I'd open another tab, answer another message, anything to prove I was still moving.

It took me years to realise that the discomfort wasn't laziness — it was simply withdrawal from a lifetime addiction to busyness.

But who wrote that rule? Who decided that sitting quietly in the *chair of clarity* was less noble than running in circles?

The answer is older than you think.

It wasn't biology. It wasn't logic.

It was industry — the perfect marriage between guilt and profit.

The Birth of a Useful Lie

When time became measurable, life became taxable.

Clocks, factories and faith joined forces to make stillness a sin.

In medieval Europe, idleness was condemned as spiritual decay. By the Industrial Revolution, it had become an economic crime.

The first factory managers realised something powerful: a rested worker was a dangerous worker — one who might start asking questions.

So "busy" became the new "good", and "rest" became "lazy".

The phrase *time is money* may have built empires, but it quietly dismantled peace.

Why We Still Worship Busyness

Centuries later, we still bow to the cult of productivity.

Our worth is measured in emails sent, calories burned, notifications cleared.

We fill every silence with scrolling, every pause with purpose.

Psychologist Adam Grant calls this *"the urgency trap"* — the illusion that moving fast equals moving forward.

And neuroscientist Andrew Huberman explains that the brain's attention systems are designed for rhythm, not continuity.

In other words: even your neurons want a break.

Yet we keep sprinting through life as if stillness were something to apologise for.

The Irony of the Lazy Genius

History, of course, disagrees with this hysteria.

Some of the most productive minds were masters of strategic idleness.

Bill Gates famously retreats twice a year for his *Think Week* — reading, staring, walking.

Churchill defended his daily nap as "indispensable to statesmanship."

Even modern tech leaders now schedule "no-meeting days" to think, not to perform.

Perhaps laziness, when deliberate, is just wisdom that's learned how to pace itself.

The Science of Stillness

Research from Harvard and Stanford continues to confirm what intuition always whispered:

moments of idleness reactivate the brain's **default mode network** — the system that links creativity, problem-solving and emotional regulation.

In simple terms, doing nothing is how the brain does everything.

Your body, too, knows the rhythm: effort, rest, renewal.

Ignore those cycles and stress takes over the controls.

What culture calls laziness, biology calls maintenance.

Reclaiming the Right to Pause

Conscious laziness isn't apathy.

It's respect — for time, for body, for thought.

It's the ability to say, *"I'll wait until this makes sense,"* instead of *"I'll do it because everyone else is."*

It's the courage to sit in the chair of clarity and let the noise tire itself out.

Laziness, practiced with intention, is the quiet rebellion that keeps your humanity intact.

Lazy Exercise #1 – Busting the Myth

Next time you catch yourself feeling guilty for resting — notice it.

Who's talking: your body, or your calendar?

If it's your body, listen.

If it's your calendar, smile politely and ignore it.

You've just performed your first act of productive laziness.

[Lazy Dialogue →]

You've sat still long enough to see the myth unravel.

Now let's learn to tell the good kind of laziness from the kind that quietly drains us.

Chapter 2

Good Laziness vs. Harmful Laziness

If laziness were a food, it would come in two flavours: the nourishing kind that restores you — and the greasy kind that leaves you heavy and regretful.

The trouble is, society threw them both into the same basket and labelled it *"bad."*

That's like blaming all food because of doughnuts.

But laziness, like any instinct, isn't the enemy — it's a compass.

The *lazy compass* doesn't tell you what to avoid.

It tells you **where energy doesn't want to go**.

 The Two Faces of Laziness

There's **good laziness** — the kind that pauses, reflects, recharges.

And there's **harmful laziness** — the kind that avoids,

delays, numbs.

The first saves energy for what matters.

The second wastes it on guilt and escape.

Daniel Kahneman, Nobel laureate and professional observer of human overthinking, would call this a "System 1 vs. System 2" conflict.

Your instinct wants rest; your ego wants applause.

And when they argue, the result is confusion that looks suspiciously like procrastination.

But not all procrastination is bad.

Psychologist Piers Steel, who's spent decades studying the science of delay, discovered something unexpected:

people who postpone tasks often perform better — if they delay *with purpose*.

That's not laziness; that's timing.

So maybe laziness isn't a vice — it's an untrained sense of rhythm.

The Case for Good Laziness

Good laziness is rest chosen with intention.

It's the moment you close the laptop before your thoughts start looping.

It's walking away from a problem long enough for your subconscious to solve it.

Neuroscience backs this up:

when you stop forcing focus, your brain's **default mode network** connects loose ideas into insights.

That's why your best thoughts show up in the shower, not in a meeting.

Good laziness doesn't resist life — it synchronises with it.

The Trap of Harmful Laziness

Then there's the other flavour — the one that starts sweet and ends sour.

Harmful laziness isn't rest; it's escape.

It's the quiet agreement between fatigue and fear that says, *"Maybe tomorrow."*

Scrolling for hours, eating when you're not hungry, overthinking instead of deciding — all feel like activity, but none create renewal.

This type of laziness drains instead of restores.

It numbs the present and borrows energy from the future.

The lazy compass wobbles here — not because it's broken, but because you stopped checking the map.

How to Tell the Difference

Here's the test:

After a lazy moment, do you feel lighter or heavier?

Good laziness clears your head.

Harmful laziness fills it with static.

Good laziness is a pause.

Harmful laziness is a pause you forget to end.

The Subtle Art of Self-Pacing

Real mastery lies not in constant drive, but in adjusting speed consciously.

Musicians don't play at full volume all the time.

Painters leave empty space on the canvas.

The consciously lazy do the same with their lives.

As productivity researcher Cal Newport puts it, "Focus without rest is fragile."

The smartest workers don't push harder; they protect their attention.

Good laziness isn't slowing down — it's staying calibrated.

The Guilt Mirage

Many people don't suffer from laziness. They suffer from guilt.

We've been taught that comfort equals failure.

That rest is indulgence.

But guilt doesn't build character; it just wastes time.

You don't need to earn rest — you're built for it.

So next time guilt whispers, "You should be doing something,"

remember: *doing nothing well is something rare.*

 Lazy Exercise #2 – The Half-Intent Rule

For the next few days, observe how you rest.

Each time you stop, ask:

"Am I resting *to recharge*, or *to avoid*?"

If you're not sure, do half of whatever you planned.

Nap half the time, scroll half the feed, reply to half the messages.

You'll be amazed how often "half" is already enough.

[Lazy Dialogue →]

You've learned to listen to your lazy compass.

Now let's explore what happens when science itself begins to agree with it.

Chapter 3

The Science of Slowing Down

Modern life runs on the illusion of acceleration.

We measure success by how much we can fit into a day, how quickly we can move between screens, tasks, or thoughts.

But the human body — and the mind that rides inside it — is still wired for the rhythm of the *slow river*.

Push the current too fast, and the water turns cloudy.

Slowing down isn't a luxury. It's maintenance.

And as every scientist who studies performance eventually discovers, **the brain was never designed for speed — it was designed for rhythm.**

The Biology of the Brake

Inside every twenty-four-hour day, your body runs smaller, hidden cycles called **ultradian rhythms** — 90-minute waves of energy and recovery.

Neuroscientist Andrew Huberman explains that after roughly an hour and a half of focused effort, our neural chemistry shifts.

Dopamine and acetylcholine — the drivers of concentration — begin to fall, and cortisol quietly takes the wheel.

If you ignore that signal, your brain doesn't reward you with more focus. It punishes you with fatigue, irritation, and shallow thought.

Slowing down isn't laziness; it's neurological respect.

Matthew Walker, sleep researcher at Berkeley, found that even short breaks increase long-term retention by up to 30%.

Rest doesn't steal productivity — it secures it.

The Flow Paradox

Psychologist Mihaly Csikszentmihalyi spent decades studying what he called *flow* — that state where time dissolves and you feel both effort and ease.

His discovery was simple yet radical:

You can't enter flow by force. You enter it by rhythm.

Flow happens when challenge meets calm.

Not panic, not boredom — but that narrow riverbank between them.

The *slow river* of attention needs boundaries, not barriers.

Too much control and you freeze; too little and you drift.

The consciously lazy person floats right in the middle, using energy like an artist mixes paint — with awareness.

When Thinking Becomes Noise

The modern brain is rarely quiet.

It's constantly reacting — to notifications, headlines, voices, plans.

We confuse motion with meaning.

But research at Harvard's Department of Psychology revealed that **a wandering mind isn't a distracted mind**.

It's often a creative one.

The brain's "default mode network" — active during rest and daydreaming — integrates memories, emotions, and ideas in the background.

That's why the solution to many problems arrives when you stop searching for it.

So if someone catches you staring out the window, call it by its scientific name: *unstructured cognitive integration*.

Speed Is a Form of Fear

We rush not because time is short, but because silence is long.

Busyness feels safer than stillness.

You can't question your direction when you're running too fast to look around.

But slow isn't the opposite of fast.

It's the opposite of empty.

To slow down is to choose depth over display — to move

through life like a diver, not a sprinter.

Nature's Reminder

Every system in nature works in cycles of effort and rest.

The tide withdraws before returning.

Seasons pause before blooming again.

Even the heart itself beats in waves of contraction and release.

We are not meant to be exceptions to this law.

When you honour your rhythm, you don't fall behind the world — you stop tripping over it.

Lazy Exercise #3 – The 90-Minute Rule

Try working or creating in waves instead of marathons.

Set no timer — just pay attention to when your focus fades.

That's your signal to pause, breathe, or walk.

Think of your day as a series of *slow rivers* instead of highways.

You'll still arrive — you'll just enjoy the scenery.

[Lazy Dialogue →]

You've learned to flow with your own rhythm.

Now let's look at those who mastered this long before neuroscience had a name for it.

Chapter 4

What History's Geniuses Really Knew About Laziness

Every generation thinks it invented exhaustion.

Yet history is full of brilliant people who did their best work between long pauses.

They understood something we've forgotten: genius doesn't sprint — it strolls.

They didn't fear stillness; they built with it.

In an age that treats quiet as unproductive, it's worth remembering that **the world's greatest breakthroughs often began at a standstill — under the window of stillness.**

Aristotle: Walking Slowly Toward Wisdom

More than two thousand years ago, Aristotle taught philosophy not from a desk, but on long, unhurried walks.

His students called themselves the *Peripatetics* — "the ones who stroll."

To Aristotle, thinking was a movement of the body as much as the mind.

Wisdom, he believed, needs rhythm.

You walk, you pause, you observe.

No timer, no rush — just the gentle pace of clarity.

Somehow, civilisation advanced for millennia on that principle, until the clock arrived and we stopped looking where we were going.

Leonardo da Vinci: The Productive Procrastinator

Centuries later, Leonardo da Vinci perfected what we now call *strategic idleness*.

He started dozens of projects, abandoned most of them, and yet changed the course of science and art.

Historians often called him distracted. But neuroscientists today would call him incubating.

His mind wandered by design.

Leonardo wrote: *"Men of lofty genius sometimes accomplish the most when they work the least."*

He painted slowly because he was busy seeing.

His apparent laziness was simply precision in disguise.

Haruki Murakami: The Modern Slow Routine

Fast-forward to the 21st century, and Japanese novelist Haruki Murakami — author of marathon-length books — lives by a paradoxically lazy discipline.

He wakes at four, writes for five hours, runs or walks, then spends the rest of the day doing nothing.

No emails, no meetings, no digital distractions.

"I repeat the same routine every day," he says. "To me, repetition is the key to creativity."

Murakami understands what Aristotle and Leonardo already knew:

Slowness is not the enemy of brilliance; it's its ecosystem.

The Pattern They Shared

Different centuries, same insight:

Every one of these minds protected space for stillness.

They all understood that creativity blooms not from pressure but from permission.

Modern neuroscience agrees.

Research from the University of British Columbia found that people who alternate between focus and rest generate more original ideas than those who focus continuously.

Rest isn't the opposite of creation — it's the architecture beneath it.

Our Modern Amnesia

We've inherited the results of their wisdom but not the rhythm that made it possible.

We admire their art but reject their habits.

We expect brilliance at the speed of Wi-Fi.

Maybe it's time to re-learn what they never forgot:

that *the window of stillness* — that open, waiting space where thought can breathe — is not a luxury, it's a tool.

You can't see new ideas if your mind never stops moving.

Lazy Exercise #4 – The Genius Pause

Today, find your own "window of stillness."

Sit by an actual window, if possible.

No phone, no music, no plan.

Look at something simple — a tree, the sky, the world not asking for anything.

If inspiration shows up, fine.

If not, you've already succeeded.

[Lazy Dialogue →]

You've learned from the masters of deliberate idleness.

Next, let's look not at history, but at nature — and how laziness became the most reliable survival skill on Earth.

Chapter 5

Laziness as a Survival Skill

We tend to think of laziness as a weakness.

But evolution seems to think otherwise.

If the goal of life is survival, then every efficient species — every creature that wastes nothing — is not lazy but intelligent.

And we humans, despite our gadgets and calendars, still run on that same ancestral code.

Hidden beneath guilt and caffeine lies one of the oldest biological truths:

the lazy instinct isn't your flaw — it's your safeguard.

Nature's Default Setting

In the wild, no creature moves all the time.

Lions rest twenty hours a day.

Whales alternate hemispheric sleep to survive.

Trees go dormant each winter, saving their strength for bloom.

In evolution, rest is not optional — it's strategy.

Darwin observed that the species that survive aren't the strongest or fastest, but the most *adaptive*.

And adaptation, by definition, means conserving energy until the moment it matters.

Humans once lived by that rhythm — hunt, eat, rest, repeat.

But then came the factory, the office, the digital feed.

Now we "hunt" constantly and forget to recover.

We've replaced survival with simulation.

The Energy Economy

Economists have a saying: *resources that never rest, deplete.*

It applies just as much to nations as to nervous systems.

Modern productivity culture tells us to maximise every minute.

But biology measures success differently — in balance, not burnout.

Harvard studies on recovery show that periods of deliberate rest increase long-term performance more than continuous effort.

It's called **adaptive energy allocation** — the art of doing less, smarter.

Olympic athletes already know this.

Roger Federer's training schedule includes as much rest as play.

He calls it "letting the body learn without forcing it."

Even in business, the pattern holds.

Warren Buffett — perhaps the world's laziest billionaire in the best sense — spends up to 80% of his workday reading and thinking.

His strategy: *"I don't look for more things to do. I wait for the right things to come to me."*

That's not apathy. That's precision.

When the Lazy Instinct Saves You

Your body sends quiet alerts before collapse.

Fatigue, impatience, distraction — these are early messages from your *lazy instinct* saying, *"Pause now or pay later."*

But instead of listening, we drown them in espresso and call it motivation.

At Stanford, neuroscientists studying burnout found that ignoring fatigue triggers the brain's threat response, shrinking access to the prefrontal cortex — the part responsible for reasoning and creativity.

Translation: when you fight your lazy instinct, you become stupider.

Conscious laziness, on the other hand, keeps you efficient by design.

It's nature's way of saying: *"You have one battery — use it wisely."*

Strategic Laziness in Action

In the animal kingdom, every act of brilliance is preceded by stillness.

The cheetah doesn't chase every gazelle. It waits for the right one.

That pause isn't indecision; it's mastery.

Humans call it timing.

Economists call it optimisation.

The lazy call it Tuesday.

If you know when to stop, you're already halfway to wisdom.

The Science of Slowing to Survive

Biologists at Harvard and Stanford have found that the nervous system alternates between *sympathetic* (action) and *parasympathetic* (recovery) states — a built-in see-saw of effort and rest.

Disregard that balance long enough, and your body revolts: insomnia, anxiety, irritability — all symptoms of energy mismanagement.

Laziness is not the disease; it's the body's early cure.

From Biology to Philosophy

The *lazy instinct* is evolution's most misunderstood gift.

It's the quiet intelligence that keeps you alive, creative, and sane.

Ignoring it is like driving a car without oil — you'll go faster only until you don't.

The consciously lazy don't chase every opportunity. They choose the meaningful ones.

They don't treat stillness as surrender. They treat it as survival.

You're not failing when you rest.

You're performing nature's oldest trick: conserving strength for the right fight.

Lazy Exercise #5 – The Energy Audit

At some point today, pause and notice:

What drains you? What restores you?

Don't overthink it — your body already knows.

The trick is to listen before it shouts.

If that feels too philosophical, take the lazy shortcut:

do nothing, and see what your energy decides to do next.

[Lazy Dialogue →]

You've learned how survival itself prefers slowness.

Now let's explore how doing absolutely nothing can become not just natural — but an art form.

Chapter 6

The Art of Doing Nothing Without Guilt

There's a kind of silence that doesn't feel empty — it feels alive.

You know it when you sit still long enough for the world to continue without you, and instead of panic, you feel peace.

That silence is where the mind finally lands when it stops running.

It's what I call *the empty chair* — the space you occupy when you stop performing your life and start inhabiting it.

Doing nothing, consciously, is the most underestimated art of all.

Why Doing Nothing Feels So Hard

We live in a world allergic to pauses.

Every gap must be filled — with sound, motion, or validation.

Even meditation has become something to optimise.

But as philosopher Blaise Pascal wrote centuries ago,

"All of humanity's problems stem from man's inability to sit quietly in a room alone."

He said that before emails, smartphones, and notifications — before guilt had Wi-Fi.

Doing nothing feels wrong because we've been conditioned to believe that value only exists in motion.

But the opposite is true: motion without meaning is how we lose ourselves.

The Empty Chair

The *empty chair* is not literal — though you might want to find one.

It's the symbol of conscious presence.

When you sit without intention, something subtle happens: you start noticing what your thoughts do when nobody's watching.

At first, they complain. Then they slow down.

And finally, they dissolve into something quieter — awareness without commentary.

That's not laziness. That's coming home.

The Science of Stillness

Modern mindfulness research, led by neuroscientist Judson Brewer at Yale, shows that the brain in rest mode displays *less noise and more order.*

Areas linked to anxiety calm down, while creativity and emotional regulation increase.

In other words, when you "do nothing," your brain does its best work.

Stillness restores coherence — a kind of inner harmony that doesn't depend on achievement.

It's not mystical; it's neurological.

The Permission to Pause

The consciously lazy person no longer asks permission to rest — they *give* it.

They understand that guilt is just the ghost of old conditioning.

You don't need to justify a pause.

You only need to allow it.

Nothing collapses when you stop moving.

Quite the opposite: things begin to align.

As Zen teacher Thich Nhat Hanh said,

"Doing nothing is doing something very important — it's allowing."

Lazy Exercise #6 – The Empty Chair Practice

Find a chair — any chair.

Sit for five minutes, or two, or until you start smiling at the absurdity of sitting for no reason.

You don't have to breathe a certain way or think a certain thing.

Just stay long enough for guilt to leave the room before you do.

You'll know it worked when you start hearing your own thoughts as if they belonged to someone gentle.

[Lazy Dialogue →]

You've learned how stillness restores order inside the mind.

Now let's look at the body — and the secret rhythm hidden in its favourite rebellion: the afternoon nap.

"Never mistake motion for progress."
— Ernest Hemingway

"Half of life is knowing what to leave undone."
— Harry L. Nikula

Chapter 7

Afternoon Naps – The Secret Power Source

In a world that glorifies sleepless ambition, the nap is an act of quiet rebellion.

It's the shortest, most elegant protest against the cult of fatigue.

You close your eyes not to escape life, but to return to it with precision.

If there's a symbol for the *Lazy Revolution,* it's this:

the nap as a revolution — small, soft, and unapologetically human.

The Science of the Siesta

NASA once studied pilots on long-haul missions and discovered something remarkable:

a 26-minute nap improved alertness by 54% and performance by 34%.

That's not magic; that's biology reclaiming its rhythm.

During a nap, your brain performs a system reboot — clearing adenosine, consolidating memory, and balancing the nervous system.

It's the body's built-in energy upgrade, available free of charge.

And yet, we treat it like a crime.

The Western Nap Taboo

Somewhere between the factory and the office, the nap was exiled.

The Protestant work ethic declared sleep sacred only at night.

Daytime rest became a sign of weakness — a moral defect wrapped in a pillow.

But while Western offices banned naps, entire cultures built around them thrived.

In Spain, the *siesta* is a tradition.

In Japan, *inemuri* — the "sleeping while present" — is considered dedication, not laziness.

The world's longest-living communities, from Sardinia to Okinawa, all rest midday as part of their routine.

They nap not because they're tired, but because they're wise.

The Political Power of Rest

Winston Churchill napped daily during World War II.

He called it "the half-day holiday."

It wasn't indulgence; it was strategy.

"When the war begins again after my nap," he wrote, "I will be ready."

Modern entrepreneurs are slowly rediscovering the same principle.

Arianna Huffington built an entire company around sleep advocacy after collapsing from exhaustion.

Her conclusion was simple: *"Sleep your way to the top — literally."*

Even Silicon Valley — birthplace of the all-nighter — now installs nap pods.

Revolution, it seems, happens horizontally.

The Neurochemistry of Renewal

While you nap, the brain produces slow-wave activity that clears out waste proteins and stabilises emotional balance.

It's like defragmenting a hard drive made of feelings.

Short naps (10–30 minutes) increase dopamine and serotonin levels — the same chemicals associated with creativity and calm.

That's why great thinkers from Einstein to Dalí used

"micro-naps" to refresh the mind without falling into deep sleep.

Dalí even held a key in his hand as he drifted off; when it fell, the sound woke him at the perfect creative moment.

He called it "the slumber with a key."

Your phone has never offered a better feature.

The Lazy Logic Behind the Nap

A nap doesn't steal time; it stretches it.

Half an hour of stillness can turn eight hours of dull effort into four hours of sharp clarity.

The consciously lazy person doesn't nap because they're exhausted.

They nap because they understand compound interest — in energy.

Each pause multiplies focus, resilience, and emotional bandwidth.

It's not a waste of time; it's a redistribution of intelligence.

How to Nap Like a Lazy Genius

Forget sleep apps, eye masks, or perfectly curated ambient playlists.

The art of napping is about permission, not precision.

1. Find a quiet place — or don't.
2. Lie down — or just close your eyes.
3. Aim for twenty minutes — or less.

The goal isn't to sleep; it's to stop trying.

If you wake up, good.

If you don't, also good.

You can't fail a nap.

Lazy Exercise #7 – The Strategic Snooze

At any point today, declare a "half-hour holiday."

You don't need a bed, just surrender.

If you can't nap, rest your eyes.

If you can't rest, stop pretending you're fine.

When you wake up — or don't — notice how the world looks softer, slower, almost reasonable again.

That's not laziness.

That's maintenance.

[Lazy Dialogue →]

You've reclaimed the nap as strategy.

Now let's see what happens when you apply the same principle to how you begin your days — with less friction, fewer decisions, and a wardrobe that does half your thinking for you.

Chapter 8

Dress Simple, Think Less

Mornings are overrated.

Not because they arrive too early — but because they demand too many decisions before your brain has even clocked in.

What to wear.

What to eat.

What to answer first.

Which version of yourself to be today.

By the time most people leave home, they've already made more choices than a chess player in mid-game.

And then they wonder why they're tired before lunch.

That's where **the morning shortcut** begins:

simplify what doesn't matter so you can focus on what does.

The Fashion of Efficiency

Barack Obama once said he only wears grey or blue suits.

"I'm trying to pare down decisions," he explained. "I don't want to waste energy choosing clothes."

Steve Jobs did the same — black turtleneck, jeans, sneakers.

A uniform not of vanity, but of sanity.

It's not about style. It's about cognitive conservation.

Psychologist Roy Baumeister called it *decision fatigue* — the gradual depletion of willpower through trivial choices.

Each small decision drains the same mental battery that powers creativity, patience, and focus.

By simplifying the first hour of your day, you preserve energy for the ones that matter.

Simplicity as a Superpower

Simplicity isn't plainness — it's precision.

It's not caring less; it's caring selectively.

When you remove friction from your mornings, you remove noise from your mind.

You give yourself back the luxury of clarity before the world starts shouting.

The consciously lazy person understands that every extra option is an invitation to waste attention.

They curate their mornings like an artist arranges light —

with purpose, not perfection.

The Psychology of Routine

Research from Duke University found that up to 45% of daily actions are habitual.

That means almost half your life runs on autopilot — whether you designed it or not.

Conscious laziness simply means choosing what goes on that autopilot.

It's building systems that work for you, not the other way around.

You don't need to be creative about breakfast or brilliant about socks.

Save originality for something that deserves it.

The Morning Shortcut in Practice

Here's the lazy formula:
- Keep one part of your morning identical every day.
- Let the rest unfold.

The repetition becomes a kind of meditation.

You no longer "get ready" — you just begin.

The best part? Nobody will notice.

Because simplicity looks a lot like confidence.

Minimal Effort, Maximum Presence

The lazy genius isn't obsessed with efficiency.

They're obsessed with peace.

When you stop making small, meaningless decisions, you create space for slow coffee, quiet thoughts, and mornings that feel like mornings — not pre-meetings.

Clarity isn't found in doing more.

It's found in needing less.

Lazy Exercise #8 – The Morning Shortcut

Tomorrow, simplify one thing.

Pick your clothes tonight.

Or eat the same breakfast twice in a row.

Or leave your phone facedown until you've been awake for ten minutes.

If that feels revolutionary, congratulations — you've just hacked your own morning.

[Lazy Dialogue →]

You've dressed your thoughts in simplicity.

Now let's step outside and see how the same principle applies to everything you carry — or don't.

Chapter 9

Minimal Accessories, Maximum Freedom

The world is noisy, even when it's silent.

We collect, decorate, and accumulate — convinced that every new thing adds identity.

But clutter doesn't reveal who you are; it hides it.

Simplicity is not the absence of style.

It's the maturity of it.

Somewhere between consumerism and chaos lives a more elegant idea:

freedom through subtraction.

The Uncluttered Mirror

Every object you own reflects a decision you once made.

And every decision leaves a trace of energy.

The *uncluttered mirror* is not just your room — it's your mind reflected outward.

When you clear space around you, you clear static inside you.

Minimalism isn't about white walls or empty shelves.

It's about being able to see yourself again — without the visual noise of everything you don't need.

The Psychology of Too Much

Psychologists from Princeton University found that visual clutter competes for your brain's attention the same way loud sounds do.

Each unnecessary object is a cognitive micro-stressor.

In short: your desk is shouting at you.

Marie Kondo may have turned decluttering into an industry, but her core idea remains timeless:

keep only what sparks clarity.

Conscious laziness adopts that logic not as a lifestyle trend, but as an emotional hygiene routine.

Every item you release returns a piece of attention to its rightful owner — you.

Designers of Simplicity

Coco Chanel once advised, *"Before you leave the house, look in the mirror and take one thing off."*

That wasn't vanity — it was philosophy.

Decades later, Apple's chief designer Jony Ive applied the same principle to technology:

"Perfection," he said, "is achieved not when there's nothing more to add, but when there's nothing more to take away."

Elegance is efficiency in disguise.

What Chanel did for accessories, Ive did for devices: both turned clarity into luxury.

The Aesthetics of Ease

True style — in clothes, spaces, or thoughts — feels effortless.

It doesn't try to impress; it invites you to breathe.

The consciously lazy person isn't anti-beauty.

They simply know that beauty without calm becomes noise.

A clean desk, an unadorned wrist, a quiet room — these are not minimalism for its own sake.

They're instruments of focus, designed to protect your peace.

When Less Becomes Enough

Freedom doesn't begin when you own nothing.

It begins when nothing owns you.

You don't have to throw everything away.

Just stop carrying what you don't remember choosing.

The *uncluttered mirror* isn't about aesthetics — it's about visibility.

It's about meeting your own reflection without interference.

Lazy Exercise #9 – The One-Thing Ritual

Today, remove one thing from your environment.

A bracelet, an app, an open tab.

Not because it's bad — because it's background noise.

Observe how silence looks when it finally has space.

You might find that clarity doesn't sparkle — it shines quietly.

[Lazy Dialogue →]

You've cleared your space and your reflection.

Now let's move to the table — where simplicity meets appetite, and rest becomes part of the menu.

Chapter 10

Eat, Rest, Repeat – A Lazy Approach to Food

We eat like we live — fast, distracted, and always reaching for the next thing.

We treat meals as pit stops, not rituals.

And then we wonder why our bodies keep asking for more while our minds feel emptier.

But food, at its best, was never meant to be fuel alone.

It was meant to be rhythm — a daily reminder that life digests better when you do.

The *slow plate* isn't about recipes. It's about presence.

The Speed Epidemic

Most people don't eat meals anymore — they refuel.

They chew while scrolling, talk while swallowing, plan while digesting.

We've turned nourishment into multitasking.

But your body doesn't multitask. It can either digest or defend.

When you eat in a hurry, your nervous system stays in survival mode — cortisol up, enzymes down.

The result? More stress, less absorption, and a strange hunger that has nothing to do with food.

Slowing down isn't indulgence. It's biology.

The Science of Savoring

Nutritionists from the University of Minnesota found that people who eat mindfully — paying attention to taste, smell, and pace — consume 25% less without feeling deprived.

Because when the brain registers flavour, it registers satisfaction.

Michael Pollan summarised it perfectly:

"Eat food. Not too much. Mostly plants."

Simple. Lazy. Profound.

And in the world's healthiest communities — the Blue Zones of Sardinia, Okinawa, and Ikaria — meals are never rushed.

People eat slowly, talk slowly, live long.

Their longevity isn't genetic; it's rhythmic.

When Food Becomes Noise

Our relationship with food mirrors our relationship with time: both are filled until they lose meaning.

We chase diets and superfoods, forgetting that digestion begins with attention.

Even water, if drunk in haste, can feel heavy.

Conscious laziness invites you to sit, breathe, and taste before you swallow — not as a ritual, but as respect.

You don't need to count calories when you count moments.

The Slow Plate Philosophy

The *slow plate* isn't a rule — it's a reminder.

To eat when you're hungry, not when you're anxious.

To stop when you're satisfied, not when you're done.

To share, because connection digests better than solitude.

When you eat slowly, time stretches.

Conversation deepens.

And even the simplest meal starts to feel like gratitude.

That's what the lazy genius knows: food doesn't just feed you — it resets you.

The Hidden Rest in Routine

There's a reason cultures that eat together tend to thrive together.

Meals mark boundaries — between work and home, effort and ease.

They remind you to pause before you burn out.

Eating well has never been about willpower.

It's about rhythm — the art of giving your body and your day the same thing: a beginning, a middle, and a rest.

Lazy Exercise #10 – The Slow Plate

At your next meal, eat as if time didn't exist.

No phone. No background noise.

Chew. Taste. Notice.

If someone asks what you're doing, tell them: "digesting existence."

Then smile — it's half a joke, half a truth.

[Lazy Dialogue →]

You've learned to rest while eating.

Now let's move your attention from the table to the body itself — and discover how motion can be lazy without being still.

Chapter 11
Move Like a Lazy Genius: Effort, Ease and Energy

The modern world has a strange definition of movement.
It celebrates sweat, strain, and steps counted by machines — as if effort alone were proof of life.
But the body has a quieter philosophy.
It prefers rhythm to performance, balance to punishment.
To move like a lazy genius is to stop treating your body like a project and start treating it like a partner.
Not a machine, but a conversation.

The Wisdom of Motion

Friedrich Nietzsche, who walked miles every day through the Swiss Alps, wrote that *"all truly great thoughts are conceived while walking."*
He understood what modern neuroscience has confirmed: movement isn't separate from thought — it *creates* it.

When you move gently, your brain releases endorphins and neurotrophins — chemicals that improve focus and emotional balance.

Movement becomes meditation.

Exercise turns into thinking.

You don't need a gym for that. You just need a direction.

From Discipline to Dialogue

We've been trained to treat the body as an employee — something to manage, correct, or exhaust.

But movement is not compliance; it's communication.

Every stretch, every breath, every slow walk is your body's way of saying, *"I'm still here, and I'd like to help."*

Ignore that voice long enough, and it starts whispering in tension and pain.

Listen to it, and you discover that laziness was never the opposite of activity — only the absence of aggression.

The Rhythm of Ease

There's a kind of strength that only appears when effort disappears.

The yogic tradition calls it *sthira sukham asanam* — steadiness and comfort in motion.

Science calls it *parasympathetic regulation* — the state in which your body performs efficiently without stress.

It's the **rhythm of ease** — that place where breath, balance, and awareness move together.

It's how Roger Federer makes a 200 km/h serve look like a sigh.

Real mastery looks lazy because it no longer fights itself.

The Myth of "No Pain, No Gain"

Our culture worships struggle.

We treat soreness as achievement, burnout as glory.

But "no pain, no gain" is the battle cry of people who mistake discomfort for depth.

Biologically, pain doesn't make you stronger; recovery does.

Muscles, neurons, ideas — they all grow in rest, not in strain.

Even professional trainers know it: the best athletes spend more time recovering than pushing.

The lazy genius learns this early — not to avoid work, but to time it wisely.

Movement as Mental Hygiene

Your body doesn't just carry your brain — it cleans it.

When you move, circulation increases, oxygen rises, and cognitive fog fades.

The National Institutes of Health found that moderate movement (like walking 20 minutes a day) improves long-term memory and creativity by up to 50%.

The reason?

Your body thinks better than your thoughts do.

So, when you feel stuck, move — not to escape, but to stir the water.

Stillness Inside Motion

Stillness isn't the absence of motion; it's its perfection.

Every dancer knows it. Every athlete feels it for a second before the moment lands.

It's that pause inside the rhythm where everything aligns.

The consciously lazy person doesn't separate action from rest — they blend them.

Because balance isn't what happens between extremes; it's what happens *during* them.

Lazy Exercise #11 – The Unplanned Loop

Today, walk with no purpose.

No podcast, no destination.

Just you, your breath, and the rhythm of ease.

Notice how your thoughts follow your steps, then dissolve into quiet.

That's not unproductivity.
That's intelligence in motion.

[Lazy Dialogue →]

You've learned to move without force.

Now let's see how the same rhythm applies to words — how silence can speak louder than speech itself.

"*Simplicity is the ultimate sophistication.*"
— Leonardo da Vinci

"*Luxury, after all, is nothing but the absence of noise.*"
— Harry L. Nikula

Chapter 12

Lazy Communication: Saying More by Talking Less

The modern world suffers from verbal inflation.

Too many words, too little meaning.

We mistake volume for clarity, speed for intelligence, noise for connection.

But true communication doesn't happen in the words themselves.

It happens in **the pause between words** — that silent gap where listening begins and ego ends.

The Cult of Constant Conversation

We talk to prove existence.

We reply to feel relevant.

We fill silence before it reminds us who we are.

Social media turned monologues into metrics, and somewhere between emails and emojis, we forgot the art of being quiet.

Yet, the consciously lazy person knows this: communication is not a race to be heard — it's a rhythm to be shared.

The Brevity of Brilliance

Abraham Lincoln's Gettysburg Address lasted two minutes.

Two hundred words that outlived empires.

He spoke softly, left space between sentences, and let meaning breathe.

Because the more weight your words carry, the more silence they require to stand.

The lazy communicator doesn't use language to fill air; they use it to shape it.

They understand that restraint is not shyness — it's precision.

The Ancient Art of Silence

Centuries before microphones, Lao Tzu wrote:

"He who knows, does not speak. He who speaks, does not know."

That wasn't cynicism; it was clarity.

Speech without awareness is just movement without rhythm.

Modern neuroscience agrees: listening activates more areas of the brain than speaking.

In 2018, Harvard Business Review reported that leaders who practiced deliberate silence improved trust and team clarity by over 40%.

Turns out, silence scales better than slogans.

Why We Explain Too Much

We often believe that more words will solve the misunderstanding.

But most conflicts aren't caused by silence — they're caused by explanation fatigue.

The lazy genius asks:

– Does this need to be said?

– Does it need to be said *by me*?

– Does it need to be said *now*?

If the answer is no twice, the silence will handle it better.

The Pause Between Words

In music, the note only matters because of the silence surrounding it.

In speaking, the pause is the punctuation that makes truth audible.

The consciously lazy person uses silence as a design element — to frame thought, to cool emotion, to invite response.

You don't need eloquence to be understood.
You need presence.

Digital Noise and the Myth of Urgency

Every ping feels personal.
Every message demands a reaction.
But responsiveness is not connection; it's captivity.
The lazy communicator chooses when to be reachable.
They treat their attention as a scarce resource — because it is.
Ignoring isn't rudeness; it's self-preservation.
Silence online is the new eloquence.

The Gift of Listening

Listening lazily doesn't mean passivity.
It means softening focus, allowing words to arrive instead of chasing them.
It's waiting not for a gap to speak, but for a moment to understand.
The lazy listener doesn't fix, interrupt, or advise.
They simply make space.
And in that space, people unfold.

Lazy Exercise #12 – The Half Challenge

For half a day, say only half of what you normally would.
Cut messages in half.
Answer questions simply.
Leave stories unfinished.
Watch how silence completes the sentences for you.
Watch how people lean in when you stop overexplaining.
Half the words, double the peace.

[Lazy Dialogue →]

You've learned to speak slowly and listen fully.
Now let's look at the digital noise surrounding your silence — and learn how to stay connected without being consumed.

Chapter 13

Digital Laziness: Controlling Tech Before It Controls You

Technology was supposed to make life easier.

Instead, it made ease impossible.

We wake up inside our inboxes, eat beside our notifications, and fall asleep under the blue light of other people's urgency.

We've built an empire of convenience that keeps us permanently busy.

And then we blame ourselves for feeling tired.

The truth is simple:

your attention is the most profitable resource on Earth — and everyone's mining it except you.

Conscious laziness begins the moment you stop digging.

The Myth of Connectivity

We mistake connection for communication, availability for presence.

The more connected we become, the less we actually connect.

MIT sociologist Sherry Turkle calls it *"the flight from conversation."*

We hide behind messages to avoid meaning.

Silence feels risky, so we drown it in sound.

But here's the paradox: the more you broadcast, the less you belong.

Digital laziness is not disconnection — it's discernment.

It's remembering that just because something pings doesn't mean it deserves your pulse.

The Quiet Screen

Imagine your screen as a window instead of a mirror.

Most people use it to reflect themselves — updates, opinions, anxieties.

The consciously lazy use it to observe — to choose what enters and what stays out.

The *quiet screen* isn't about deleting everything.

It's about designing silence inside the noise.

That might mean disabling notifications, muting group

chats, or checking messages twice a day instead of twice a minute.

It's not digital detox — it's digital diet.

Cal Newport and the Cost of Constant Access

Computer scientist Cal Newport calls this era "the attention economy,"

and his advice is both radical and lazy: *schedule boredom.*

By creating moments of intentional disconnection, you allow focus to rebuild itself.

Neuroscience confirms it — attention works like a muscle; it needs rest to recover strength.

In one Stanford study, people who multitasked regularly performed worse on every measure of attention and memory than those who didn't.

In other words: doing everything makes you worse at everything.

The lazy genius knows this and quietly opts out.

The Stoic Precedent

Even the ancients understood this problem — they just didn't have Wi-Fi.

Seneca warned that *"being everywhere is being nowhere."*

He would have hated group chats.

His point remains valid: constant input erases individuality. You cannot hear your own thoughts if you never let them finish.

To be consciously lazy online is to become selectively present — to choose depth over display.

The Modern Sabbath

Religious or not, the idea of the Sabbath — one day of intentional rest — remains one of humanity's most revolutionary time hacks.

It's not about ritual; it's about rhythm.

Try a modern version: one hour a day, or one day a week, where nothing demands your thumbs.

No notifications, no updates, no scrolling.

At first it feels like withdrawal.

Then it feels like clarity.

Eventually, it feels like coming back to yourself.

Lazy Exercise #13 – The Quiet Screen Ritual

Pick one device and silence it for the rest of the day.

If that sounds terrifying, you've just found your addiction.

Open your screen only with intention.

Ask: "Am I looking, or escaping?"

Every unanswered message is a small revolution.

[Lazy Dialogue →]

You've learned to quiet the screen.
Now let's return to the physical world — and rethink the way we work, choosing progress without the panic.

Chapter 14

The Lazy Approach to Work: Results Without the Rush

We work faster than ever and finish less than before.

We multitask, micromanage, and call it progress.

The modern office has become a theatre of exhaustion — full of people acting busy while secretly trying not to drown.

But the consciously lazy worker knows a secret the productivity gurus won't tell you:

slowing down is not a luxury — it's a competitive advantage.

That's the *unhurried edge*.

The Myth of Hustle

Somewhere in the last two decades, hard work became a religion.

We replaced Sunday sermons with Monday metrics.

We worship the calendar, sacrifice weekends, and pray to the inbox.

But hustle is not a strategy — it's panic in disguise.

The harder you chase everything, the less you catch anything.

Warren Buffett put it simply:

"The difference between successful people and really successful people is that the latter say no to almost everything."

In other words: laziness is focus refined.

Tim Ferriss and the 80/20 Reality

Entrepreneur Tim Ferriss popularised a principle the lazy have practised forever — the 80/20 rule.

Eighty percent of results come from twenty percent of effort.

The trick is to find that twenty and stay there.

The consciously lazy don't avoid work.

They avoid meaningless work.

They're selective, not idle.

They use precision where others use pressure.

The Toyota Lesson

Even factories learned this truth before offices did.

Toyota's "Kaizen" method — continuous improvement

through small, deliberate actions — is the corporate version of conscious laziness.

No rush. No chaos. No drama.

Just refinement over repetition.

It's not about speed; it's about flow.

Because efficiency without calm is just expensive anxiety.

Deep Work, Lazy Mind

Cal Newport, author of *Deep Work,* proved that the average worker spends less than three hours a day in genuine focus.

The rest is noise: emails, meetings, context-switching.

Yet those three quiet hours produce almost all real progress.

The lazy genius doesn't feel guilty for working less — they feel responsible for working *well*.

They guard their calendar like a sacred garden: only what grows there stays.

The Unhurried Edge

In an economy addicted to urgency, calm becomes currency.

The *unhurried edge* isn't about doing things slowly — it's about doing them once.

Clarity replaces chaos, and precision replaces repetition.

The consciously lazy person moves like a chess player, not a hamster.

They understand that thinking is work, and resting is strategy.

When you stop sprinting, you start steering.

The Science of the Pause

Neuroscience backs this rhythm:

our brains can sustain high-quality focus for about 90 minutes before requiring reset.

Ignoring that rhythm lowers accuracy and drains creative energy.

So, the lazy approach isn't rebellion — it's maintenance.

It's working *with* biology, not against it.

Every pause is an investment in precision.

Lazy Exercise #14 – The One-Thing Rule

Tomorrow, choose one task — the one that actually matters — and do only that until it's done.

Ignore the rest. Don't even pretend to multitask.

By noon, you'll have achieved more than most people do by Friday.

And with less coffee.

[Lazy Dialogue →]

*You've learned to work without hurry.
Now let's look at the other side of productivity — money — and discover how laziness can turn finance into freedom.*

Chapter 15

Money the Lazy Way: Simplifying Finances

Money isn't evil. It's just loud.

It shouts numbers, deadlines, comparisons — and we keep shouting back, trying to win an argument nobody ever wins.

But what if peace was the real currency?

What if the goal was not to earn endlessly, but to need less?

That's the philosophy of **the quiet wallet** — money that doesn't keep you awake.

The Myth of More

The world tells us that wealth equals freedom.

But the more you own, the more you manage.

And management is the opposite of rest.

Economist Morgan Housel wrote: *"The hardest financial skill is getting the goalpost to stop moving."*

Because once your life becomes a scoreboard, it never ends — just restarts at a higher level of stress.

The consciously lazy person plays a different game: stability over status, clarity over accumulation.

They understand that not wanting everything is the quickest path to feeling rich.

Naval Ravikant and the Philosophy of Enough

Entrepreneur and philosopher Naval Ravikant said,

"If you can't be happy with a coffee, you won't be happy with a yacht."

That isn't moralising; it's mathematics.

The equation of peace has fewer variables.

Lazy wealth isn't about having nothing — it's about having *nothing to prove.*

It's the kind of financial calm where every pound has a purpose and no purchase feels like panic.

The *quiet wallet* doesn't chase. It circulates.

The FIRE Misunderstanding

The FIRE movement — Financial Independence, Retire Early — became the dream of a generation tired of corporate captivity.

But many who reach it find themselves trapped in a different loop: obsessing over optimisation, frugality, and fear of loss.

Because freedom isn't just the absence of a boss — it's the absence of financial anxiety.

Conscious laziness doesn't worship spreadsheets.

It redefines wealth as the ability to choose slowness without guilt.

The Psychology of Spending

Harvard behavioural studies show that money spent on *time* — not things — increases happiness significantly.

Hiring help, reducing commute, buying rest — these are the lazy genius investments.

Every pound you spend is a vote for the life you want.

Spend wisely, not widely.

The consciously lazy invest in systems that simplify, not in objects that complicate.

When Simplicity Becomes Strategy

You don't need complex portfolios to find peace.

You need clarity.

Automate what repeats.

Eliminate what distracts.

Save quietly, give generously, live light.

The *quiet wallet* is not minimalist by deprivation — it's minimalist by design.

It's money that moves like water, not like weight.

The Freedom Formula

Freedom = Expenses < Peace of Mind.

If you earn more but feel anxious, you're not richer — just busier.

If you need less but sleep better, congratulations: you've retired early without leaving work.

Lazy Exercise #15 – The Quiet Audit

Look at one recurring expense — not to cut it, but to ask: "Does this serve my peace?"

If yes, keep it.

If not, cancel it — not out of guilt, but out of gratitude.

Every unnecessary payment is just noise you no longer need to hear.

[Lazy Dialogue →]

You've simplified your finances and bought back your peace.
Now let's explore how the same clarity applies to something far more complex — love, relationships, and human connection.

Chapter 16
Relationships Made Easy: Love Without Overcomplication

Love was never supposed to feel like multitasking.

And yet, most modern relationships resemble inboxes — full, reactive, and slightly overdue.

We've confused intensity with intimacy, availability with affection, explanation with connection.

But the consciously lazy know that love doesn't need constant maintenance — it needs **space to breathe.**

That's the secret of **the calm orbit** — two people moving around a shared centre of ease, not control.

The Myth of Constant Effort

We've been told that love requires constant work — daily effort, scheduled talks, emotional performance.

But anything that needs permanent fixing was never built

on stillness.

Therapist Esther Perel says, *"Love rests on the twin pillars of closeness and space."*

Too much closeness kills desire; too much distance kills connection.

Lazy love lives in the middle — caring deeply without clutching tightly.

Alain de Botton and the Art of Imperfection

Philosopher Alain de Botton calls love *"our best opportunity to be generous rather than fair."*

In other words: don't keep score.

We often measure affection in hours, texts, or gestures, as if intimacy were a spreadsheet.

But relationships don't need constant measurement — they need presence.

Lazy communication (from Chapter 12) becomes essential here:

listen slowly, speak less, assume good intent.

When you stop over-explaining, connection starts breathing again.

Carl Rogers and Unconditional Positive Regard

Psychologist Carl Rogers proposed one of the simplest and hardest ideas in human connection:

"Give people the freedom to be themselves, and they often become better versions of it."

That's the calm orbit — not control, not detachment, but faith.

You stay near without managing, love without editing, trust without supervision.

It's the relationship equivalent of a steady pulse: effortless, reliable, human.

The Quiet Courage of Not Fixing

We're conditioned to respond, repair, react.

But sometimes the laziest thing you can do for someone is nothing — just hold the space while they find their own rhythm.

Conscious laziness in love is not avoidance.

It's respect for another person's timeline.

You don't have to solve what silence can soften.

The Calm Orbit

Healthy love isn't fusion; it's gravity.

Two complete bodies moving in their own paths, held together by understanding, not obligation.

When love becomes an orbit, not a rescue mission, it starts to feel like home again.

Lazy Exercise #16 – The Unsent Reply

Next time you feel the urge to respond instantly — to defend, explain, correct — don't.

Wait an hour. Or a day.

Let silence answer for you.

If the connection is real, it will survive the pause.

If it isn't, you've saved yourself the drama of proving it.

[Lazy Dialogue →]

You've learned that even love moves better in silence.

Now let's explore a deeper rhythm — the quiet power of waiting, and how delay can become a form of wisdom.

Chapter 17
The Wisdom of Waiting: Patience as a Lazy Virtue

We live in an age that treats waiting as weakness.

We want instant replies, instant results, instant purpose.

But nothing meaningful in life has ever arrived on time — only when we were ready to receive it.

Patience is the most misunderstood form of laziness.

It looks like stillness, but it's actually trust.

That's the secret of **the slow horizon** — learning to see beyond urgency, where things ripen in their own rhythm.

Seneca and the Luxury of Time

Two thousand years ago, the Stoic philosopher Seneca wrote:

"To be everywhere is to be nowhere."

He wasn't talking about travel — he was describing impatience.

The busy man, Seneca said, never really lives anywhere, because he's always rushing toward the next thing.

The consciously lazy person takes the opposite approach: they let time work for them, not against them.

Waiting isn't wasted when it's observed.

Alan Watts and the River of Becoming

Philosopher Alan Watts compared life to music: you don't play a song to finish it faster — you play to enjoy its unfolding.

Modern life, however, has turned every melody into a race.

We rush through meals, conversations, even sunsets, chasing an arrival that never arrives.

The *slow horizon* reminds us that clarity comes from continuity, not haste.

You can't rush sunrise. You can only wake up for it.

The Science of Delayed Reward

In the 1970s, psychologist Walter Mischel conducted the famous Stanford "marshmallow experiment."

Children were given one marshmallow with a promise: wait fifteen minutes, and they'd get two.

Those who waited went on, statistically, to live calmer,

more successful lives.

It wasn't about sugar.

It was about strategy — the ability to pause desire long enough for wisdom to catch up.

Patience, biologically speaking, is emotional regulation — laziness at its most intelligent.

When Waiting Becomes Vision

Most mistakes are made not from lack of effort, but from lack of pause.

We decide too soon, reply too fast, apologise too late.

The lazy genius knows that time is not an obstacle; it's an ally.

They wait not because they're indecisive, but because they respect unfolding.

Rushing is the enemy of rhythm.

And rhythm is the heartbeat of everything that lasts.

The Art of Slow Decisions

The next time you feel pressured to answer, decide, or act — try silence first.

Let the impulse cool, let your emotions complete their sentences.

Clarity often arrives disguised as delay.

Even nature knows this: fruit that ripens overnight usually

rots just as quickly.

Patience is not inaction; it's incubation.

Lazy Exercise #17 – The Slow Horizon Practice

Think of one thing you've been pushing for — a plan, a reply, a result.

Stop chasing it for one day.

Instead of asking "When will it happen?", ask "What is it teaching me while I wait?"

You might find that life has been moving all along — you just stopped noticing.

[Lazy Dialogue →]

You've discovered the wisdom of waiting.

Now let's explore its playful cousin — procrastination — and learn why delay, when conscious, can be a creative superpower.

"Leisure is the mother of philosophy."
— Thomas Hobbes

"Better £50 in the shade than £100 in the sun."
— Harry L. Nikula

Chapter 18
Positive Procrastination: Why Not Everything Must Be Urgent

Procrastination has a bad reputation.

It's been called laziness, avoidance, weakness — the intellectual equivalent of dust on ambition.

But what if delay isn't always decay?

What if postponing is sometimes *processing*?

That's the paradox of **the thoughtful delay** — the space between intention and action where clarity quietly forms.

The Cult of Urgency

Modern life worships speed.

We celebrate fast responses, fast results, fast failures — as if life were a hackathon.

But speed rarely equals success.

It often just multiplies mistakes.

The "do it now" culture confuses motion with momentum.
Yet, every great idea in history began as hesitation.
Leonardo da Vinci delayed finishing the *Mona Lisa* for sixteen years.
Newton "waited" under a tree.
Even your own thoughts need a pause before they make sense.

John Perry and the Power of Structured Delay

Stanford philosopher John Perry introduced the term *structured procrastination* — the art of putting off one thing by doing another useful thing.
It sounds absurd, but it works.
Your brain resists vague pressure but enjoys small victories.
So, when you avoid the big task by completing smaller ones, you're still moving — just horizontally, not vertically.
Procrastination, properly harnessed, becomes time's quiet assistant.

Tim Urban and the Instant Gratification Monkey

Blogger Tim Urban turned this psychology into comedy.
He described the *"Instant Gratification Monkey"* — the part of your brain that avoids discomfort by chasing dopamine.
But even Urban admits that this monkey occasionally leads

you to creativity, not disaster.

Some of his best work was born from last-minute clarity — the "panic productivity" that appears only when time gets real.

That's the *thoughtful delay* in disguise: a tension that refines focus.

The Science of Productive Pausing

Cognitive psychology supports what procrastinators have always known subconsciously:

ideas incubate during rest.

In a University of Wisconsin study, people who deliberately delayed solving a problem came up with 28% more creative solutions than those who answered immediately.

The gap wasn't wasted time — it was mental composting.

Delay becomes creative when done with awareness.

You're not avoiding the task — you're letting the task evolve.

When Waiting Becomes Wisdom

The consciously lazy person doesn't fight procrastination; they collaborate with it.

They know that not every moment of inaction is avoidance — sometimes it's alignment.

If you delay with curiosity instead of guilt, the pause becomes a strategy.

If you fill it with reflection instead of scrolling, it becomes evolution.

Laziness, practiced intelligently, is patience with a plan.

The Paradox of Efficiency

You can't be "on time" for everything.

You can only be *in rhythm* with what matters.

The lazy genius doesn't rush decisions or cling to deadlines that belong to someone else's panic.

They understand that urgency is contagious — and choose not to catch it.

The *thoughtful delay* isn't an excuse to stop — it's permission to breathe before continuing.

Lazy Exercise #18 – *The Delay Test*

Pick one task you feel pressured to finish today.

Now, don't.

Wait 24 hours before touching it.

Observe what happens: clarity sharpens, relevance fades, or a better idea appears.

You'll realise that most urgencies are self-inflicted — and that a paused clock still tells time.

[Lazy Dialogue →]

You've learned that waiting can be productive. Now let's take that same principle and bring it into creativity itself — where doing less becomes the mother of invention.

Chapter 19
Creative Laziness: Innovation Through Doing Less

The greatest ideas in history were born in boredom.

Not in meetings, deadlines, or brainstorming marathons — but in the fertile silence that follows a long pause.

That's the paradox of innovation: it doesn't begin with effort, but with emptiness.

Creativity thrives not when we force it, but when we *forget* to chase it.

This is **the fertile pause** — the still space where imagination grows without supervision.

The Myth of Constant Creativity

Modern creativity is over-engineered.

We build co-working spaces, hold "idea sessions," and caffeinate our imagination to death.

But great ideas don't respond to noise.

They respond to neglect.

Pablo Picasso once said, *"Inspiration exists, but it has to find you resting."*

He painted slowly, often leaving canvases unfinished for years, waiting for the next moment of clarity.

He didn't force genius; he waited for it to return home.

Brian Eno and the Art of Deliberate Accident

Musician and producer Brian Eno — the mind behind David Bowie's and U2's most famous albums — built his career on controlled laziness.

When creativity stalled, he'd shuffle cards from his *Oblique Strategies* deck: cryptic phrases like *"Honour your error as a hidden intention."*

He understood what every lazy genius learns eventually: creativity isn't a factory; it's a field.

You can't harvest ideas all year. You have to let the soil rest.

The *fertile pause* is that rest — deliberate, curious, unhurried.

Google's 20% Rule

Even corporations, built on spreadsheets and deadlines, have rediscovered the power of idleness.

Google once allowed engineers to spend 20% of their

workweek on any project they chose.

The result? Gmail, AdSense, and a culture of experimentation that paid better than control.

Freedom, not pressure, breeds invention.

The same principle that fuels art fuels algorithms: time off-task is time well invested.

The Science of Incubation

Cognitive psychologists describe creativity as a four-stage cycle: preparation, incubation, illumination, and verification.

Most people skip the second stage — incubation — because it looks suspiciously like laziness.

But during that pause, the unconscious mind keeps rearranging ideas in silence.

It's why solutions appear in the shower, in the car, or mid-nap.

The *fertile pause* isn't absence of activity — it's invisible activity.

Doing Less, Seeing More

Creativity doesn't reward busyness; it rewards awareness.

The lazy artist doesn't rush drafts — they let intuition do the editing.

The lazy thinker doesn't chase originality — they wait until simplicity reveals something truer.

In a world obsessed with productivity, imagination needs permission to idle.

The Fertile Mindset

You don't have to create constantly to be creative.

You just have to stay available.

The truly innovative mind works like a cat — alert, relaxed, waiting for inspiration to walk by.

The consciously lazy person understands that not every pause is procrastination.

Some pauses are beginnings in disguise.

Lazy Exercise #19 – The 20% Rule (at Home)

This week, give one day — or one hour — to something delightfully unproductive.

A sketch, a tune, a thought, a walk.

No goals, no plans, no monetisation.

Just the fertile pause.

If an idea visits, thank it.

If not, thank yourself for remembering what quiet feels like.

[Lazy Dialogue →]

You've learned that creation loves quiet.
Now let's take that calm curiosity and carry it out into the world —
not to escape it, but to wander through it differently.

Chapter 20

The Lazy Traveler: Seeing the World Without Stress

Some people travel to escape life.

The consciously lazy travel to meet it more slowly.

In an age of cheap flights and expensive burnout, movement has become another form of consumption — places ticked off like emails.

But travel, like thought, loses meaning when rushed.

You don't need more destinations.

You need **the still journey** — the art of arriving without running.

The Cult of Constant Motion

We move because stopping feels scary.

We pack schedules into vacations, chase sunsets as if they're appointments, and return home more tired than when we left.

The modern traveller doesn't cross borders — they skim them.

Every experience becomes a selfie, every moment a caption.

But what's the point of seeing the world if you never let it see you?

Pico Iyer and the Geography of Stillness

Essayist Pico Iyer, who has lived and written in airports, calls stillness "the ultimate luxury."

He says travel is not about movement, but awareness — *"a way of standing still."*

Iyer's philosophy echoes the lazy truth:

you don't travel to change places, but to change pace.

The world doesn't need to be conquered; it needs to be observed.

And sometimes the deepest discovery is found from the same chair, with the phone switched off.

Alain de Botton and the Art of Slow Seeing

Philosopher Alain de Botton reminds us that travel is not an escape from routine, but an opportunity to *see routine anew*.

In *The Art of Travel,* he notes that airports, train stations,

and hotel rooms are mirrors for our own restlessness.
The lazy traveller doesn't rush the itinerary.
They collect atmospheres instead of stamps.
They measure distance in silence, not in miles.

The Science of Awe

A 2018 Stanford study found that people who regularly experienced *awe* — moments of vastness that expand perspective — reported greater calm and life satisfaction.
The key wasn't exotic landscapes; it was attention.
A walk in your neighbourhood, if seen slowly, can be as transformative as a sunrise over Bali.
Because awe doesn't require travel — it requires *presence*.

The Lazy Map

Imagine a map not made of places, but of pauses:
the café where you watched rain without checking your phone,
the park bench where you forgot time,
the view you didn't photograph because you were too busy enjoying it.
That's the geography of the lazy traveler — the still journey that never ends, because it happens wherever you are.

Lazy Exercise #20 – The Unplanned Walk

Take a walk with no destination.

No playlist, no app, no pace goals.

If you see something beautiful, don't capture it — describe it in your head.

When you return, don't post about it.

Let it exist only in memory.

Some beauty is meant to stay offline.

[Lazy Dialogue →]

You've travelled the world without leaving calm behind.

Now let's explore the hardest kind of journey — the one at home — where patience becomes parenting and simplicity becomes care.

"There is more to life than increasing its speed."
— Mahatma Gandhi

"The revolution starts with a nap."
— Harry L. Nikula

Chapter 21

Lazy Parenting: Raising Kids Without Burnout

Modern parenting looks like a full-time job without weekends.

We track milestones, curate playdates, optimise nap schedules, and call it love.

But children don't need perfect parents — they need present ones.

And presence begins where exhaustion ends.

That's the quiet brilliance of **the patient mirror** — the idea that your calm, not your control, shapes your child's world.

The Performance Trap

Parenting has become performance art.

Every snack, school, and sentence feels like a competition.

We scroll through highlight reels of other people's families and forget that real connection is rarely photogenic.

The consciously lazy parent rejects this theatre.

They understand that *doing less for your child often means being more with them.*

Attention, not activity, is what children remember.

Maria Montessori and the Power of Observation

Over a century ago, educator Maria Montessori built an entire philosophy on one radical idea:

children learn best when adults interfere the least.

Her classrooms were designed for independence — chairs they could move, tools they could choose, space they could own.

Montessori didn't call it laziness.

She called it *trust.*

The lazy parent follows the same rule: step back so they can step forward.

Gabor Maté and Emotional Presence

Psychologist Gabor Maté reminds us that children don't need constant entertainment; they need *attunement* — emotional resonance with a calm adult.

Stress, he explains, is contagious. But so is serenity.

When you slow down, your nervous system teaches theirs

how to rest.
Your stillness becomes their safety.
In that sense, laziness isn't neglect — it's regulation.
You can't raise calm humans if you never show them what calm looks like.

The Harvard Study on Attunement

A longitudinal study from Harvard University found that consistent presence — not perfect parenting — predicted long-term emotional resilience in children.
Parents who practiced "responsive pauses" before reacting to misbehaviour raised kids with better emotional control.
That pause is the *patient mirror* in action: reflection before reaction.

The Gift of Boredom

The modern parent fears boredom like a virus.
But boredom is the birthplace of imagination.
When kids say, "I'm bored," they're not broken — they're ready to create.
The lazy parent doesn't rush to fill every silence.
They let curiosity find its own entertainment.
Because the goal of parenting isn't to raise busy children — it's to raise balanced adults.

The Calm Household

A lazy household isn't messy; it's rhythmic.

Mornings aren't marathons. Evenings aren't negotiations.

It's a place where time is generous and affection unhurried.

When rules come from peace, they rarely need to be repeated.

Children grow into the tone of the home — not its speed.

Lazy Exercise #21 – The Pause Before the Answer

Next time your child asks a question or makes a mistake, pause before you react.

Let your face rest, let your breath land.

Then answer softly — or not at all.

Sometimes silence is the most educational sound.

[Lazy Dialogue →]

You've learned how calm leads better than control.

Now let's take that same principle into the wider world — from family to leadership — where the best guide is often the one who moves the least.

Chapter 22

The Lazy Leader: Guiding Without Micromanaging

The modern workplace is full of motion, but starved of meaning.
Leaders chase results, hold endless meetings, send urgent emails, and call it vision.
But motion isn't leadership — it's choreography.
Real leadership doesn't shout. It listens, adjusts, and trusts.
It's the art of doing less, but meaning more.
That's **the steady hand** — guidance without grip.

The Myth of the Hyperactive Leader

We've been conditioned to admire the leader who never sleeps, never stops, never blinks.
But exhaustion doesn't inspire; it intimidates.
Simon Sinek, author of *Leaders Eat Last,* explains that great leaders create safety, not stress.

Their job isn't to be omnipresent — it's to be *predictably calm.*

The lazy leader embodies that calm.

They know that stability is contagious.

People don't follow intensity; they follow steadiness.

Satya Nadella and the Power of Empathy

When Satya Nadella became CEO of Microsoft, he didn't double production targets or increase pressure.

He introduced empathy as a core value.

Meetings became shorter, hierarchies flatter, and innovation flourished.

Nadella once said, *"Our ability to learn is more important than our ability to know."*

That's the steady hand in motion — guiding through humility, not command.

Lazy leadership isn't passive.

It's quietly transformative.

The Patagonia Principle

Yvon Chouinard, founder of Patagonia, built one of the world's most respected companies by stepping back.

He trusted his employees, limited bureaucracy, and publicly declared, *"Let my people go surfing."*

That sentence is the lazy leader's creed.

Freedom is not the opposite of responsibility — it's how responsibility becomes sustainable.

Patagonia thrived not because it worked harder, but because it worked with integrity and rest.

The Science of Delegation

Neuroscience shows that autonomy — the feeling of being trusted — activates the same reward centres as financial gain.

When leaders micromanage, they trigger anxiety; when they delegate with confidence, they trigger motivation.

Conscious laziness is the leader's version of trust.

It's the pause before interference, the question before correction, the calm before chaos.

The steady hand directs from stillness.

The Paradox of Presence

The best leaders are often invisible.

Their absence isn't neglect; it's empowerment.

Their teams grow not because they're pushed, but because they're allowed.

The lazy leader doesn't lead from above or ahead — they lead from alongside.

They understand that influence without pressure lasts longer than authority enforced by fear.

Lazy Exercise #22 – The Pause Before the Order

Tomorrow, resist the urge to give one instruction.
Instead, ask a question: "What do *you* think?"
Then wait.
Watch competence unfold when it's not interrupted.
You'll discover that most people don't need direction — just space.

[Lazy Dialogue →]

You've led with calm and watched chaos shrink.
Now let's scale that idea beyond offices and families — to society itself — and see how a lazy revolution might just fix a culture addicted to busyness.

Chapter 23
Society and the Lazy Revolution: Rethinking Productivity Culture

Every generation thinks it's working harder than the one before.

But maybe we're just spinning faster.

We've built an economy that treats exhaustion as virtue and stillness as sin.

We measure human worth by output and call collapse "dedication."

And yet, the more we produce, the emptier we feel.

The problem isn't that we're lazy.

It's that we've forgotten how to rest together.

That's the essence of **the collective breath** — a society that pauses not out of weakness, but wisdom.

The Myth of Infinite Motion

Modern culture runs on the illusion of endless growth.

Every metric must rise, every quarter must outperform the last, every person must "hustle."

But infinite motion is only sustainable for machines.

Humans, on the other hand, are cyclical beings — they bloom, rest, and renew.

Economist Rutger Bregman calls this *"the tyranny of efficiency."*

He argues that shorter workweeks and slower living don't just improve well-being — they *strengthen economies.*

Less fatigue, more focus. Less work, more worth.

Jenny Odell and the Art of Refusal

Artist and writer Jenny Odell wrote a book called *How to Do Nothing* — not as escapism, but as protest.

She argues that attention has become the new currency, and reclaiming it is a political act.

To do nothing consciously is to say no to systems that profit from your exhaustion.

It's the modern equivalent of planting a tree in the middle of a traffic jam — small, slow, subversive.

The lazy revolution isn't about quitting society; it's about redesigning it.

Carl Honoré and the Slow Movement

Journalist Carl Honoré, author of *In Praise of Slow*, once confessed that he tried to read his son a "one-minute bedtime story" to save time.

That absurd moment woke him up to the insanity of speed.

He started a global movement around slowness — in food, parenting, business, and thought.

Because a society that moves slower doesn't regress; it evolves sustainably.

Speed is impressive only until it breaks something irreplaceable.

The Economics of Enough

If growth were the answer, we'd all be happy by now.

Instead, we're richer in tools but poorer in time.

Our productivity apps keep track of everything except joy.

Conscious laziness invites a different metric:

How much peace did this produce?

How much meaning survived the meeting?

The lazy revolution doesn't aim to stop the world — just to let it catch its breath.

The Collective Breath

Imagine a society that pauses — collectively.
A city that moves slower on purpose.
A workday that ends before people forget why they began.
The collective breath is not rebellion; it's recovery.
It's a civilisation remembering its pulse.
When people breathe together, noise becomes rhythm.

Lazy Exercise #23 – The Shared Pause

Find one moment this week to pause — with others.
At work, at home, on a call.
No productivity, no agenda, no explanation.
Just breathe together, even for ten seconds.
You'll feel it: the brief, beautiful silence of a world that hasn't forgotten itself.

[Lazy Dialogue →]

You've helped the world slow down for a moment.
Now let's turn inward — toward gratitude, stillness, and the quiet freedom that arrives when doing less becomes being more.

Chapter 24
Lazy Nirvana: Gratitude in Stillness

There's a silence that doesn't ask for attention — it simply exists.

It doesn't perform calmness or promise enlightenment.

It just *is*.

That silence is **lazy nirvana** — the moment when doing nothing stops being resistance and starts being gratitude.

You don't reach it.

You remember it.

The Lazy Sun

Every morning, the sun rises slowly, without urgency, without noise.

It doesn't need motivation quotes or to-do lists.

It simply shines, and the world arranges itself around its rhythm.

That's the lazy sun: patient, predictable, powerful.

It reminds us that consistency doesn't require speed, and light doesn't compete with darkness — it replaces it naturally.

You don't have to chase brilliance; you just have to stop running from it.

Eckhart Tolle and the Power of Presence

Spiritual teacher Eckhart Tolle wrote, *"Realize deeply that the present moment is all you ever have."*

It's a statement so simple it sounds lazy — and that's exactly the point.

Gratitude is the language of presence.

When you slow down enough to notice, even breathing feels like success.

Lazy nirvana isn't a destination — it's a pace.

A way of existing without demanding constant justification.

Thich Nhat Hanh and the Art of Breathing

Zen master Thich Nhat Hanh once said, *"Smile, breathe, and go slowly."*

Few sentences have ever summarised conscious laziness better.

His practice wasn't about escape, but engagement — meeting life as it is, without over-editing it.

To breathe slowly is to say, *"I'm here."*
To smile while doing it is to say, *"That's enough."*

The Gratitude Equation

Gratitude + Stillness = Contentment.

It's a formula that can't be optimised, monetised, or measured.

You can't fake it or schedule it.

You can only notice it — like warmth from the lazy sun.

The more you try to hold it, the faster it fades.

The more you relax into it, the longer it stays.

The Return to Enough

Lazy nirvana isn't about transcendence.

It's about returning to enough — that soft, unremarkable place where your needs and your peace finally shake hands.

It's when the pursuit ends and presence begins.

When you stop trying to earn what was already yours: time, breath, and the right to be still.

Lazy Exercise #24 – The Lazy Sun Moment

Once a day, find a moment of light — morning, afternoon, or candle flame.

Look at it for one full minute.

Don't name it, photograph it, or chase meaning.
Just notice that it's there — shining without rush.
Then remember: so can you.

[Lazy Dialogue →]

You've found peace in the slow glow of being.
Now let's lift our gaze once more — beyond the personal, toward the collective horizon — and imagine what a world built on calm could become.

Chapter 25

The Future Belongs to the Lazy: A New Vision for Living

If the last century belonged to speed, the next one will belong to rhythm.
The age of acceleration has reached its limit — attention is exhausted, minds are overheated, and time itself feels compressed.
But beneath the noise, something quieter is emerging.
A new intelligence — slower, wiser, softer.
That's the future of the consciously lazy:
a civilisation that learns to move at the speed of meaning.

The End of the Hustle Era

For decades, we were told that busyness was proof of value.
We built economies of exhaustion and called them progress.

But as burnout became a global epidemic, the illusion cracked.

People began to realise that the race had no finish line — only endless laps.

The next revolution won't come from louder voices or faster machines.

It will come from calm minds reclaiming their rhythm.

From Efficiency to Essence

Productivity culture worshipped efficiency.

But efficiency without reflection is just elegant chaos.

The new luxury is essence — knowing what truly deserves your energy.

Carl Honoré calls this "the slow fix" — solving problems by understanding them, not rushing them.

The consciously lazy aren't rebels; they're reformers.

They replace ambition with alignment.

They trade pressure for precision.

Rutger Bregman and the New Economics of Time

Rutger Bregman once imagined a world with a fifteen-hour workweek.

It sounded utopian — until technology made it possible, and culture refused to catch up.

The tools for freedom exist; what's missing is permission.

And that's where the lazy revolution begins — not with rebellion, but with refusal:

refusal to equate exhaustion with importance, urgency with worth, noise with value.

The lazy future isn't idle.

It's intentional.

The Slow Horizon

Imagine a horizon that doesn't recede when you walk — it waits.

That's the *slow horizon* — the vision of a future that values depth over display.

In that world, work ends when meaning does, rest isn't shameful, and calm is the new competence.

Children grow without panic, leaders guide without noise, and societies measure success by the quality of their collective breath.

That future is not far away.

It's one quiet decision away — yours.

The Lazy Sun Rises Again

The lazy sun still rises, every morning, at its own pace.

It doesn't check analytics or compete for reach.

It just shines, because that's what it does best.
So can we.
If the 20th century taught us to run, maybe the 21st will teach us to rest —
not as escape, but as evolution.

Lazy Exercise #25 – The 1% Slower Rule

Tomorrow, do everything 1% slower.
Eat, speak, reply, walk.
Nobody will notice — except you.
And that's how revolutions begin: quietly, and then everywhere.

[Lazy Dialogue →]

You've seen the horizon.
You've slowed down enough to hear the rhythm beneath the noise.
The world outside is still spinning — let it.
Revolutions don't always need manifestos;
sometimes they need a glass of something red,
a chair that doesn't ask for your posture,
and a song that forgets to end.
Before we continue, take a moment.
Don't read — listen.

Don't plan — taste.
Don't chase the future — sip it.
Because every idea, even the lazy ones,
deserves a toast and a tune.

"Don't push the river. It flows by itself."
— Fritz Perls

"The moment you stop chasing motivation, it quietly sits next to you."
— Harry L. Nikula

Bonus Chapter X
The Gentle Art of Indulgence: A Glass of Good Wine

(The Slow Glass)

There's a reason revolutions never start in gyms.

They start at tables — slowly, with laughter, over a second glass of something that asks for no explanation.

Conscious laziness has its rituals, and one of them is this: pouring a drink not to escape the world, but to taste it.

This is **the slow glass** — an invitation to sit, sip, and let the moment breathe before you do.

The Philosophy of a Glass

Wine, at its best, is distilled time.

It teaches patience: years in barrels, months in silence, seconds on the tongue.

It doesn't hurry; it ripens.

That's why the lazy genius loves it — it mirrors everything

we believe in.
Maturity without rush. Depth without noise.
The art of drinking slowly is the art of existing fully.

How to Drink Like a Lazy Philosopher

1. **Choose curiosity over price.**
   Expensive bottles aren't wiser; they're just louder.

2. **Never drink to escape.**
   Drink to arrive — into yourself, into conversation, into calm.

3. **Share it.**
   A glass alone is contemplation; a glass shared is communion.

4. **End before excess.**
   Leave a little in the bottle. Let restraint taste better than indulgence.

Lazy Pairings for the Slow Glass

Because even revolutions deserve good taste:

Mood	Wine	Moment
Reflection	Rioja Reserva (Spain)	for reading under warm light

Gratitude	Pinot Noir (France / Oregon)	when time feels kind
Soft laughter	Barbera d'Asti (Italy)	for small talk that turns real
Summer idleness	Albariño (Spain)	when windows are open and thoughts wander
Quiet night	Malbec (Argentina)	for writing, or not writing at all

(Optional substitute: good tea counts too. The lazy spirit doesn't discriminate.)

Lazy Exercise #X – The 10-Minute Glass

Pour a drink.

Set a timer for ten minutes.

Do nothing but taste. No screens, no agenda.

Watch how time expands — and how rarely you allow yourself to be this present.

The slow glass isn't about the wine. It's about the permission.

[Lazy Dialogue →]

You've tasted time in a glass.

Now let's listen to it — softly, rhythmically, the soundtrack of a world that finally remembers to rest.

Bonus Chapter Y

If You Laze, Laze in Style: The Soundtrack of Conscious Laziness

(The Lazy Playlist)
Every revolution has a rhythm.
Ours just happens to be slower — and in tune.
Music is the universal permission slip to do nothing beautifully.
It fills the room without asking for performance, reminds you to breathe without demanding attention, and makes time sound like it's smiling.
That's **the lazy playlist** — a soundtrack not for working, but for being.

Morning Calm – Waking Without Alarm

Mornings don't need motivation — they need melody.
Start soft. No drums. No rush.

Let your body remember what waking used to feel like before urgency became a ritual.

Recommended listening:
- Ludovico Einaudi – *Nuvole Bianche*
- Ólafur Arnalds – *Near Light*
- Norah Jones – *Sunrise*
- Nick Drake – *Pink Moon*
- Khruangbin – *White Gloves*

Best paired with silence, sunlight, and the smell of something warming.

Afternoon Drift – The Lazy Pulse

There's a rhythm between focus and nap — a tempo only the lazy can hear.

This is where your mind loosens its tie,

where creativity stops sprinting and starts strolling.

Recommended listening:
- Tom Misch – *It Runs Through Me*
- Zero 7 – *Destiny*
- Rhye – *Open*
- Kings of Convenience – *Cayman Islands*
- Chet Baker – *Almost Blue*

Best paired with open windows, unplanned thoughts, or the nap that saves the day.

Twilight Ease – The Slow Conversation

Evening is not for catching up; it's for catching breath.
Play something that invites dialogue, not distraction.
Let the room dim naturally; let voices soften.

Recommended listening:

- Cigarettes After Sex – *Apocalypse*
- Sade – *By Your Side*
- Angus & Julia Stone – *Santa Monica Dream*
- José González – *Heartbeats*
- The Cinematic Orchestra – *To Build a Home*

Best paired with the wine from Bonus X and someone who doesn't rush their sentences.

Midnight Stillness – Breathing in the Dark

Night isn't silence; it's the softest form of sound.
Music here shouldn't wake you — it should dissolve you.

Recommended listening:

- Max Richter – *On the Nature of Daylight*
- Nils Frahm – *Says*
- Agnes Obel – *Riverside*
- Brian Eno – *An Ending (Ascent)*
- Sigur Rós – *Samskeyti*

Best paired with low light, slow breath, and no plans to wake up early.

Lazy Exercise #Y – The One-Song Pause

Choose one song.
Sit. Do nothing until it ends.
No phone, no multitasking — just let the sound fill you completely.
You'll rediscover what silence between notes feels like — the heartbeat of the lazy revolution.

[Lazy Dialogue →]

You've listened long enough to hear what silence sounds like.
Music faded, but rhythm stayed — slower, deeper, wiser.
The lazy revolution was never only about stopping.
It was about choosing *where* to stop.
Now that you've tasted calm and heard its melody,
it's time to learn the oldest lesson of all —
that comfort, not conquest, is the real currency.
Some call it modesty.
We call it the shady principle.

Bonus Chapter Z

The Shady Principle: Better £5 in the Shade Than £10 in the Sun

Every culture has its myths of glory.
Ours just happens to sweat more than most.
We glorify the grind, the glow, the spotlight —
but nobody talks about the sunburn.
The shady principle says something simple:
peace is worth more than pride.
Better £5 in the shade than £10 in the sun.

The Sun Tax

Modern life is a solar economy.
We work under a constant glare — deadlines, exposure, performance.
Everyone wants to "shine," even when the heat starts to hurt.

Anne Helen Petersen, in her book *Can't Even,* calls this "the burnout generation":

people so desperate to be visible that they forget how to see.

The problem isn't the light itself.

It's forgetting that light, unbalanced, blinds.

Marcus Aurelius, the philosopher-emperor, warned about this two thousand years ago:

"Nothing is worth doing pointlessly or in the wrong season."

But we live in permanent summer —

and the modern workplace has become a beach with no shade.

The Shade Economy

The consciously lazy person trades differently.

They know that every bit of peace costs something,

and they're happy to pay.

They work less but last longer.

They earn less but lose less of themselves.

Their profits are measured in mornings without alarms and evenings that don't blur into email.

In the shade economy, success is not what you show, but what you *save:*

energy, time, clarity.

While others chase solar panels of productivity, the lazy genius builds a veranda.

The Wisdom of Enough

There's a dignity in stopping early.
In choosing the smaller paycheck that buys bigger quiet.
In leaving the party before the noise replaces the music.
"Enough" isn't a limitation — it's a design choice.
It's the point where quality replaces quantity,
where warmth replaces heat.
Harvard Business Review once noted that people who prioritise "recovery time" in their workweek
end up 30% more creative and 50% less likely to quit.
It seems the shade doesn't just soothe — it sustains.
So maybe the lazy revolution isn't about retreating.
It's about relocating — to the part of life where comfort and clarity share a table.

Lazy Exercise #Z – The Shade Test

Next time you're offered a brighter deal
a bigger salary, a faster project, a louder role
pause and ask:
"How much sun comes with it?"

If the answer is "too much,"
step back into the shade.
It's cooler there.
And you'll still be rich — in all the ways that count.

[Lazy Dialogue →]

You've sat in the shade and realised something the busy world forgot

peace has a price, and it's always worth paying.

You've learned to slow the body, soften the mind, and measure wealth in quiet hours.

Now, all that remains is to give these discoveries a name

to turn pauses into principles,

and rest into revolution.

Not through slogans, but through stillness.

Not by marching, but by staying.

The Language of the Lazy

Every revolution has its language.
Ours speaks softly — in chairs, naps, and light.
The Lazy Sun – the symbol of steady clarity.
It doesn't chase the horizon; it simply shines where it stands.
It reminds us that radiance needs rhythm.

The Chair of Clarity – a quiet seat of awareness.
It is where ideas arrive uninvited, and where stillness becomes intelligence.

The Nap as Revolution – the courage to pause in a world that applauds exhaustion.
It is the manifesto written on a pillow: rest is not escape, it is preparation.

The Shady Principle – better £5 in the shade than £10 in the sun.
It is the wisdom of moderation, the choice of comfort over spectacle, the art of staying cool while others burn.

The Slow Fire – the warmth that lasts longer than ambition.
It is passion without hurry, energy that flows, not explodes.

The Lazy Orchestra – the harmony of minimal effort and maximal meaning.
Each instrument plays only when necessary, and silence is part of the score.

The Chair, the Shade, the Nap – the holy trinity of the conscious lazy.
Together they form a philosophy of presence: to see clearly, rest wisely, and live gently.

The Shadow Economy of Energy – the unseen savings account of stillness.
Every quiet moment deposits strength for later. The laziest minds are often the richest.

The Warm Light – where thought replaces noise, and clarity replaces speed.
It is the light that rests, not burns.

The Lazy Sunset – the moment between doing and being, where endings stop pretending to be failures.
It is the calm that follows courage.

The Slow Architecture of Thought – the patient construction of inner balance.

Each pause is a brick; each breath, a blueprint.

The Power of Doing Less – the final metaphor, and the simplest one.

To subtract until what remains finally feels alive.

A lazy word is never empty.

It rests just long enough to mean something.

The Conscious Lazy Manifesto

(Instead of a Conclusion)

We Believe

We believe that life is not a race but a rhythm.
That rest is not retreat but return.
That silence can say more than speech,
and stillness can move the world more gently than noise ever will.
We believe that time is not money — it's meaning.
That doing less is not giving up,
but giving space for what truly matters to appear.
We believe that the lazy are not weak,
but wise enough to stop when everyone else forgets how.

We Refuse

We refuse to worship busyness.
We refuse to treat exhaustion as a badge of honour.
We refuse to measure our worth in speed,

or our success in spreadsheets.
We will not confuse productivity with purpose,
nor movement with progress.
We will not apologise for breathing before answering.

We Practice
We practice the nap as revolution.
The pause as punctuation.
The slow horizon as vision.
We choose to dress simply, eat slowly, move gently, and lead calmly.
We choose depth over display, rhythm over rush, and meaning over metrics.
We practice the art of stopping before breaking,
and of smiling at the noise as it passes by.

We Remember
That trees stand still for decades and change the air.
That lions rest twenty hours a day and remain kings.
That the lazy sun still rises — without hurry, without fail.
And so will we.

We Begin
Not with thunder, but with a collective breath.
Not with slogans, but with silence.
Not tomorrow, but now — slowly.
Because the future belongs to the lazy.

And the revolution has already begun —
one pause at a time.

Final Words

If you've reached this page, you've already slowed down.
You read, you paused, you maybe smiled — and in a world obsessed with rushing, that's an act of quiet rebellion.
This book was never meant to change your life overnight.
It was meant to give you permission to stop chasing it.
To remind you that calm is not the absence of ambition, and that stillness is not idleness — it's clarity in disguise.
You don't need to start a revolution.
You just need to continue one — the one that begins each time you choose peace over panic, rhythm over rush, meaning over motion.
If you remember nothing else, remember this:
life isn't asking you to do more.
It's asking you to notice more —
the sound of your own breath,
the light that doesn't hurry,
the simplicity that was waiting for you all along.

Thank you for reading slowly.
Thank you for being part of this quiet movement.
Now close the book.
Take a deep breath.
And let the lazy sun do the rest.

"Rest is not idleness."
— John Lubbock

"When you finally stop rushing, life starts whispering."
— Harry L. Nikula

Epilogue
The Power of Doing Less

(The Quiet Mastery)

There's a point where effort becomes elegance.

Where doing less stops looking like hesitation and starts looking like wisdom.

That's the quiet power of the consciously lazy — they don't run from the world; they walk through it without wasting motion.

The myth said that laziness was weakness.

But weakness is scattering your strength in too many directions.

Laziness, in its highest form, is focus — knowing what not to do, what not to chase, what not to say.

The Chair of Clarity

Somewhere in this book, you might have imagined a chair. The one you sit in when you finally stop pretending to be busy.

That chair isn't made of wood or time — it's made of perspective.

From it, everything slows into place:

the work that matters, the people who stay, the hours that finally belong to you.

The chair of clarity is not a throne.

It's a seat of surrender.

The Quiet Mastery

Mastery is not endless progress — it's rhythm learned so deeply it looks like rest.

The dancer who seems still before the leap.

The craftsman who pauses longer than he carves.

The mind that doesn't need to prove it's thinking.

In a world obsessed with beginnings, the lazy master celebrates pauses.

Because every pause, handled well, becomes a doorway to precision.

The fewer steps you take, the cleaner the path.

From Ambition to Attention

Ambition is loud.

Attention is lasting.

You don't need to want everything — just to notice what

already wants you.

Doing less doesn't mean you lack drive; it means you've stopped driving yourself.

The lazy genius doesn't retire from life.

They simply stop negotiating with it.

The Return to Rhythm

The revolution was never about doing nothing.

It was about doing the right amount — beautifully.

The lazy sun still rises.

The slow horizon still waits.

And somewhere, between the two, there's you — sitting in your chair of clarity, breathing at the speed of sense.

That's not the end of the book.

It's the beginning of your rhythm.

Printed in Dunstable, United Kingdom